50 Best German Cheese Recipes

By: Kelly Johnson

Table of Contents

- Käsespätzle
- Obatzda
- Flammkuchen mit Käse
- Käsekuchen (German Cheesecake)
- Maultaschen with Cheese
- Schinken-Käse-Toast (Ham and Cheese Toast)
- Kartoffelgratin mit Käse
- Quarkbällchen
- Raclette (German-style)
- Cheese-Stuffed Pretzels
- Cheese and Leek Soup
- Käsesuppe mit Hackfleisch
- Käsefondue (German-style)
- Wurstsalat mit Käse
- Käsige Frikadellen
- Bauernfrühstück mit Käse
- Käse-Schinken-Röllchen

- Zwiebelkuchen mit Käse
- Camembert im Blätterteig
- Käse-Pilz-Pfanne
- Kartoffelpuffer mit Käse
- Käsige Rösti
- Quarkauflauf
- Gekochter Käse mit Zwiebeln
- Grillkäse mit Gemüse
- Laugenstange mit Käse überbacken
- Käseknödel
- Cheese-Stuffed Bratwurst
- Käse-Hack-Auflauf
- Käse-Lauch-Brot
- Kohlrabi mit Käse überbacken
- Käse-Nudeln
- Brötchen mit geschmolzenem Käse
- Käsige Kartoffelsuppe
- Lauch-Käse-Quiche
- Leberkäse mit Käse

- Käse-Curry-Wurst
- Zucchini mit Käsefüllung
- Blätterteigschnecken mit Käse
- Paprika mit Käse überbacken
- Sauerkrautauflauf mit Käse
- Käsige Gemüsepfanne
- Rahmkäse mit Schnittlauch
- Toast Hawaii mit Käse
- Spiegelei mit Käse überbacken
- Semmelknödel mit Käse
- Kürbis-Käse-Gratin
- Hackbällchen mit Käsefüllung
- Käsige Nudelpfanne
- Käsige Zucchini-Küchlein

Käsespätzle (Cheese Spaetzle)

Ingredients:

- 2 cups flour
- 4 eggs
- 1/2 cup milk or water
- Salt
- 1 tbsp butter
- 1 ½ cups grated Emmental or Bergkäse
- 2 onions, thinly sliced

Instructions:

1. Mix flour, eggs, milk, and salt into a sticky dough.
2. Press dough through a spaetzle maker into boiling salted water. Cook until spaetzle float; drain.
3. Sauté onions in butter until deeply golden.
4. Layer spaetzle and cheese in a baking dish, top with caramelized onions.
5. Bake at 375°F (190°C) for 10–15 minutes or until cheese is melted. Serve warm.

Obatzda (Bavarian Cheese Spread)

Ingredients:

- 200g ripe Camembert or Brie
- 100g cream cheese
- 1 tbsp butter
- 1/2 tsp paprika
- 1 tbsp beer (optional)
- 1 small onion, finely chopped
- Salt, pepper, caraway seeds (optional)

Instructions:

1. Mash cheeses and butter together until smooth.
2. Mix in paprika, onion, beer, and seasoning.
3. Chill for 1 hour. Serve with pretzels or rye bread.

Flammkuchen mit Käse (Tarte Flambée with Cheese)

Ingredients:

- Flammkuchen dough (or thin pizza dough)
- 1/2 cup crème fraîche
- 1/2 onion, thinly sliced
- 100g bacon, diced
- 100g grated cheese (Gruyère or Emmental)
- Salt, pepper

Instructions:

1. Preheat oven to 475°F (245°C).
2. Roll dough very thin and place on baking tray.
3. Spread crème fraîche, top with onions, bacon, and cheese.
4. Bake 10–12 minutes until crisp and golden.

Käsekuchen (German Cheesecake with Quark)

Ingredients:

- 200g flour
- 100g sugar
- 100g butter
- 1 egg (for crust)

Filling:

- 500g Quark
- 200g sugar
- 3 eggs
- 1 tsp vanilla extract
- 1 tbsp cornstarch
- Zest of 1 lemon

Instructions:

1. Mix crust ingredients, press into springform pan base.
2. Blend filling ingredients and pour over crust.
3. Bake at 350°F (175°C) for 50–60 minutes. Cool completely before slicing.

Maultaschen with Cheese

Ingredients:

- Maultaschen (store-bought or homemade pasta pockets)
- 1 cup shredded cheese (Allgäuer Bergkäse or Emmental)
- Butter, herbs

Instructions:

1. Boil Maultaschen in salted water until cooked.
2. Drain and place in baking dish.
3. Sprinkle cheese over, dot with butter and herbs.
4. Bake at 375°F (190°C) until bubbly and golden.

Schinken-Käse-Toast (Ham & Cheese Toast)

Ingredients:

- 4 slices sandwich bread
- 4 slices ham
- 4 slices cheese (Gouda or Emmental)
- Butter or mustard

Instructions:

1. Butter or spread mustard on bread.
2. Add ham and cheese between slices.
3. Toast in a sandwich press or pan until golden and melty.

Kartoffelgratin mit Käse (Potato Gratin with Cheese)

Ingredients:

- 1 kg potatoes, thinly sliced
- 1 clove garlic
- 1 cup cream
- 1 cup milk
- 1 ½ cups grated cheese (Emmental, Gruyère)
- Salt, pepper, nutmeg

Instructions:

1. Rub baking dish with garlic.
2. Layer potatoes, season with salt and pepper.
3. Pour cream and milk over. Top with cheese.
4. Bake at 375°F (190°C) for 45–60 minutes until golden and tender.

Quarkbällchen (German Cheese Donuts)

Ingredients:

- 250g Quark
- 2 eggs
- 50g sugar
- 1 tsp vanilla sugar
- 250g flour
- 1 tsp baking powder
- Oil for frying
- Powdered sugar for dusting

Instructions:

1. Mix all ingredients into a thick batter.
2. Heat oil in a pot to 170°C (340°F).
3. Scoop small balls and fry until golden.
4. Drain on paper towels and dust with powdered sugar.

Raclette (German-style)

Ingredients:

- Raclette cheese, sliced
- Boiled potatoes
- Pickles, onions, assorted charcuterie
- Optional: paprika, mushrooms, corn, bell peppers

Instructions:

1. Arrange ingredients on platters.
2. Each person melts cheese in a raclette pan and pours it over potatoes and toppings.
3. Enjoy communally with bread and wine.

Cheese-Stuffed Pretzels (Käsegefüllte Brezeln)

Ingredients:

- Pretzel dough (homemade or store-bought)
- 1 cup shredded cheese (Emmental, Cheddar, or Mozzarella)
- 1 egg (for egg wash)
- Coarse salt

Instructions:

1. Preheat oven to 400°F (200°C).
2. Roll out dough pieces, fill the center with shredded cheese, and seal tightly. Shape into pretzels.
3. Brush with egg wash, sprinkle with coarse salt.
4. Bake for 12–15 minutes or until golden and cheese is bubbling inside.

Cheese and Leek Soup (Käse-Lauch-Suppe)

Ingredients:

- 2–3 leeks, sliced into rings
- 300g ground pork or beef (optional)
- 200g processed cheese (or cream cheese + grated cheese)
- 1 liter vegetable or chicken broth
- 1 tbsp oil
- Salt, pepper, and nutmeg

Instructions:

1. Heat oil and sauté ground meat until browned.
2. Add sliced leeks and cook until softened.
3. Pour in broth, bring to a boil, then reduce heat.
4. Stir in cheese until melted and smooth.
5. Season and simmer 10–15 minutes. Serve hot with crusty bread.

Käsesuppe mit Hackfleisch (Cheese Soup with Ground Meat)

Ingredients:

- 300g ground beef or mixed meat
- 1 onion, chopped
- 2–3 leeks, sliced
- 200g processed cheese (or melting cheese)
- 1 liter broth
- 1 tbsp oil, salt, pepper, paprika

Instructions:

1. Sauté onion and meat in oil until browned.
2. Add leeks, cook 5 minutes.
3. Pour in broth, simmer 10 minutes.
4. Stir in cheese, melt completely, and season to taste.
5. Optional: add cream for richness.

Käsefondue (German-Style Cheese Fondue)

Ingredients:

- 300g Emmental
- 300g Bergkäse or Gruyère
- 1 clove garlic
- 1 cup dry white wine
- 1 tbsp cornstarch
- 1 tsp lemon juice
- Fresh bread cubes, boiled potatoes, veggies

Instructions:

1. Rub fondue pot with garlic.
2. Heat wine with lemon juice, then slowly stir in grated cheese.
3. Dissolve cornstarch in a little wine and add to thicken.
4. Stir constantly until smooth.
5. Serve with bread and dippables.

Wurstsalat mit Käse (Sausage Salad with Cheese)

Ingredients:

- 300g sliced sausage (Lyoner or Fleischwurst)
- 150g Emmental cheese, julienned
- 1 small onion, thinly sliced
- 3 tbsp vinegar
- 2 tbsp oil
- 1 tsp mustard
- Salt, pepper, chives

Instructions:

1. Combine sausage, cheese, and onion in a bowl.
2. Whisk vinegar, oil, mustard, salt, and pepper.
3. Pour dressing over salad, mix and chill for 30 minutes.
4. Sprinkle with chives before serving.

Käsige Frikadellen (Cheesy German Meat Patties)

Ingredients:

- 500g ground meat (beef/pork mix)
- 1 egg
- 1 small onion, minced
- 1 slice bread, soaked in milk
- 100g shredded cheese
- Mustard, salt, pepper, parsley

Instructions:

1. Mix all ingredients thoroughly.
2. Form into patties and pan-fry until golden and cooked through (about 5–7 mins per side).
3. Serve with potatoes or salad.

Bauernfrühstück mit Käse (Farmer's Breakfast with Cheese)

Ingredients:

- 4 potatoes, cooked and sliced
- 1 onion, chopped
- 100g ham or bacon, diced
- 4 eggs
- 100g grated cheese
- Salt, pepper, butter/oil

Instructions:

1. Fry potatoes, onions, and ham in butter until crispy.
2. Whisk eggs, season, pour over pan contents.
3. Add cheese on top and cover until set and melted.
4. Slice and serve hot.

Käse-Schinken-Röllchen (Cheese & Ham Rolls)

Ingredients:

- 4 large slices cooked ham
- 100g cream cheese or melting cheese
- 1 tbsp chopped herbs (chives, parsley)
- Mustard (optional)

Instructions:

1. Spread cheese and herbs on each ham slice.
2. Roll up tightly and secure with toothpicks.
3. Optional: briefly bake at 350°F (175°C) for 10 minutes.
4. Serve warm or cold as a snack or appetizer.

Zwiebelkuchen mit Käse (Onion Tart with Cheese)

Ingredients:

- 250g flour
- 125ml warm water
- 15g yeast
- 2 tbsp oil
- 1 tsp salt

Topping:

- 500g onions, sliced
- 150g diced bacon
- 200g sour cream
- 2 eggs
- 150g grated Emmental or Bergkäse
- Salt, pepper, caraway seeds

Instructions:

1. Make a yeast dough: mix flour, yeast, salt, water, oil. Let rise 1 hour.
2. Sauté onions and bacon until soft.
3. Mix sour cream, eggs, cheese, and spices. Add onions/bacon.
4. Roll out dough in a baking tray, top with onion mix.

5. Bake at 400°F (200°C) for 30–35 min. Serve warm.

Camembert im Blätterteig (Baked Camembert in Puff Pastry)

Ingredients:

- 1 whole Camembert
- 1 sheet puff pastry
- 1 tbsp cranberry or fig jam
- 1 egg (for brushing)

Instructions:

1. Place Camembert in center of pastry, spread jam on top.
2. Fold pastry over to seal, trim excess.
3. Brush with egg wash.
4. Bake at 375°F (190°C) for 20–25 min until golden.
5. Serve with bread or salad.

Käse-Pilz-Pfanne (Cheese and Mushroom Skillet)

Ingredients:

- 300g mushrooms, sliced
- 1 onion, chopped
- 150ml cream
- 150g grated cheese (Gouda or Emmental)
- Butter, salt, pepper, parsley

Instructions:

1. Sauté onion and mushrooms in butter.
2. Add cream and simmer 5 minutes.
3. Stir in cheese until melted.
4. Season and garnish with parsley. Serve with bread or potatoes.

Kartoffelpuffer mit Käse (Potato Pancakes with Cheese)

Ingredients:

- 600g potatoes, grated
- 1 egg
- 1 small onion, grated
- 100g grated cheese
- 2 tbsp flour
- Salt, pepper, oil for frying

Instructions:

1. Squeeze excess liquid from grated potatoes.
2. Mix with egg, onion, cheese, flour, salt, and pepper.
3. Fry spoonfuls in hot oil until golden on both sides.
4. Serve with sour cream or apple sauce.

Käsige Rösti (Cheesy Swiss-Style Hash Browns)

Ingredients:

- 500g potatoes, cooked and grated
- 150g cheese (Appenzeller, Gruyère, or Emmental)
- 1 tbsp butter
- Salt, pepper

Instructions:

1. Mix potatoes with cheese, season.
2. Heat butter in a pan, add potato mix and flatten.
3. Fry on medium heat until golden, flip carefully, cook other side.
4. Cut into wedges and serve warm.

Quarkauflauf (German Quark Casserole)

Ingredients:

- 500g Quark
- 3 eggs
- 60g sugar
- 1 tsp vanilla
- 2 tbsp semolina or flour
- Zest of 1 lemon
- Optional: raisins or chopped apples

Instructions:

1. Mix all ingredients into a smooth batter.
2. Pour into greased baking dish.
3. Bake at 350°F (175°C) for 30–40 minutes until golden and set.
4. Serve warm with fruit or cream.

Gekochter Käse mit Zwiebeln (Cooked Cheese with Onions – Bavarian Specialty)

Ingredients:

- 250g soft cheese (e.g., Limburger or Romadur)
- 1 small onion, finely chopped
- 100ml beer or milk
- 1 tbsp butter
- Paprika, caraway seeds, salt

Instructions:

1. Melt butter in a saucepan, sauté onions.
2. Add chopped cheese and beer/milk.
3. Stir until melted and creamy.
4. Season and serve warm with rye bread.

Grillkäse mit Gemüse (Grilled Cheese with Veggies)

Ingredients:

- 2 blocks grilling cheese (e.g., Halloumi or German Grillkäse)
- Bell peppers, zucchini, onions – sliced
- Olive oil, herbs, pepper

Instructions:

1. Toss vegetables in oil and seasonings.
2. Grill veggies and cheese until golden and soft.
3. Serve together as a light meal or BBQ dish.

Laugenstange mit Käse überbacken (Cheese-Baked Pretzel Sticks)

Ingredients:

- Pretzel sticks or rolls (Laugenstangen)
- 100g grated cheese (Emmental or Cheddar)
- Optional: ham, herbs, mustard

Instructions:

1. Slice open pretzel sticks and add toppings (optional mustard and ham).
2. Sprinkle with cheese generously.
3. Bake at 375°F (190°C) for 10–12 minutes until melted and bubbly.
4. Serve warm.

Käseknödel (Cheese Dumplings)

Ingredients:

- 250g old bread, cubed
- 100g grated cheese (Emmental or Bergkäse)
- 2 eggs
- 150ml milk
- 1 small onion, finely chopped
- 1 tbsp chopped parsley
- Salt, pepper, nutmeg
- Butter for frying

Instructions:

1. Sauté onions in butter until soft.
2. Mix bread, cheese, milk, eggs, parsley, onions, and seasonings. Let rest 15 min.
3. Form dumplings with wet hands. Boil in salted water for 15–20 minutes until they float.
4. Serve with browned butter or mushroom sauce.

Cheese-Stuffed Bratwurst

Ingredients:

- 4 raw bratwursts (not pre-cooked)
- Cheese strips (cheddar, gouda, or mozzarella)
- Toothpicks or kitchen twine

Instructions:

1. Slice each brat lengthwise without cutting through.
2. Stuff with cheese, secure with toothpicks.
3. Grill or pan-fry over medium heat until cooked through and cheese is melted.
4. Serve with mustard and rolls.

Käse-Hack-Auflauf (Cheesy Ground Meat Casserole)

Ingredients:

- 500g ground beef or pork
- 1 onion, chopped
- 1 garlic clove, minced
- 250g cooked pasta or potatoes
- 200g grated cheese
- 200ml cream
- 2 eggs
- Salt, pepper, paprika

Instructions:

1. Brown meat with onion and garlic. Season.
2. Mix with pasta/potatoes and place in baking dish.
3. Combine cream, eggs, and half the cheese. Pour over.
4. Top with remaining cheese.
5. Bake at 375°F (190°C) for 25–30 min until golden.

Käse-Lauch-Brot (Cheesy Leek Bread)

Ingredients:

- 1 baguette or rustic bread, halved
- 2 leeks, sliced
- 100g cream cheese
- 150g grated cheese (e.g., Emmental)
- Butter, salt, pepper

Instructions:

1. Sauté leeks in butter until soft.
2. Mix with cream cheese and season.
3. Spread onto bread halves, sprinkle with grated cheese.
4. Bake at 400°F (200°C) for 10–12 minutes.
5. Slice and serve warm.

Kohlrabi mit Käse überbacken (Baked Kohlrabi with Cheese)

Ingredients:

- 2–3 kohlrabi, peeled and sliced
- 200ml cream
- 150g grated cheese
- Nutmeg, salt, pepper

Instructions:

1. Blanch kohlrabi slices in salted water for 5 minutes.
2. Layer in a greased baking dish.
3. Pour over cream, season with nutmeg, salt, and pepper.
4. Top with cheese and bake at 375°F (190°C) for 20–25 minutes.

Käse-Nudeln (German Mac & Cheese)

Ingredients:

- 300g cooked pasta (Spätzle preferred)
- 200g grated cheese (Bergkäse or Emmental)
- 1 onion, thinly sliced and caramelized
- Butter, pepper

Instructions:

1. Layer pasta and cheese in a casserole dish.
2. Bake at 375°F (190°C) for 15–20 minutes until bubbly.
3. Top with crispy onions and serve.

Brötchen mit geschmolzenem Käse (Melted Cheese Rolls)

Ingredients:

- 4 crusty rolls, halved
- 100g grated cheese
- Optional: tomato slices, ham, or herbs

Instructions:

1. Place cheese (and extras) on cut roll halves.
2. Bake or broil at 200°C (400°F) for 5–8 minutes until cheese is melted and golden.
3. Serve warm.

Käsige Kartoffelsuppe (Cheesy Potato Soup)

Ingredients:

- 500g potatoes, diced
- 1 onion, chopped
- 1 carrot, diced
- 1 liter broth
- 150g cheese (meltable like Gouda or Cheddar)
- 100ml cream
- Salt, pepper, nutmeg

Instructions:

1. Cook potatoes, onion, and carrot in broth until soft.
2. Purée partially, leaving some chunks.
3. Stir in cream and cheese until melted.
4. Season to taste. Serve with chives and bread.

Lauch-Käse-Quiche (Leek and Cheese Quiche)

Ingredients:

- 1 sheet puff pastry or shortcrust pastry
- 2–3 leeks, cleaned and sliced
- 200g grated cheese (Emmental or Gruyère)
- 3 eggs
- 200ml cream
- Salt, pepper, nutmeg
- Butter for sautéing

Instructions:

1. Preheat oven to 375°F (190°C).
2. Sauté leeks in butter until soft.
3. Line a tart pan with pastry and prick the base with a fork.
4. Beat eggs with cream, season with salt, pepper, and nutmeg.
5. Spread leeks and cheese over the pastry, pour egg mixture on top.
6. Bake for 30–40 minutes until set and golden.

Leberkäse mit Käse (Meatloaf with Cheese)

Ingredients:

- 600g Leberkäse (store-bought or homemade)
- 100g cheese slices (e.g., cheddar or gouda)

Instructions:

1. Preheat oven to 350°F (180°C).
2. Cut Leberkäse into thick slices and layer cheese between or on top.
3. Bake in a baking dish for 10–15 minutes until cheese is melted.
4. Serve with mustard and bread or potato salad.

Käse-Curry-Wurst (Cheesy Currywurst)

Ingredients:

- 4 Bratwursts
- 1 cup tomato ketchup
- 1 tsp curry powder
- 50g grated cheese (e.g., gouda or cheddar)
- Oil for frying

Instructions:

1. Fry or grill sausages and slice them.
2. Heat ketchup with curry powder in a small pot.
3. Pour sauce over sausage slices and sprinkle cheese on top.
4. Optional: place under broiler briefly to melt cheese.
5. Serve with fries or bread.

Zucchini mit Käsefüllung (Cheese-Stuffed Zucchini)

Ingredients:

- 2 large zucchini, halved lengthwise
- 150g cream cheese
- 100g grated cheese
- 1 garlic clove, minced
- Salt, pepper, herbs (thyme or basil)

Instructions:

1. Scoop out zucchini centers.
2. Mix cream cheese, garlic, herbs, and seasoning.
3. Fill zucchini halves with mixture, top with grated cheese.
4. Bake at 375°F (190°C) for 20–25 minutes until golden and soft.

Blätterteigschnecken mit Käse (Cheese Puff Pastry Pinwheels)

Ingredients:

- 1 sheet puff pastry
- 150g grated cheese (e.g., Emmental or mozzarella)
- 1 egg (for brushing)
- Optional: herbs, ham, or mustard

Instructions:

1. Preheat oven to 400°F (200°C).
2. Roll out pastry, sprinkle cheese and optional fillings evenly.
3. Roll up and slice into 1–2 cm thick rounds.
4. Place on a baking sheet, brush with egg.
5. Bake for 12–15 minutes until golden.

Paprika mit Käse überbacken (Cheese-Baked Bell Peppers)

Ingredients:

- 2–3 bell peppers, halved and deseeded
- 150g cottage cheese or ricotta
- 100g grated cheese
- 1 egg
- Salt, pepper, herbs

Instructions:

1. Mix cottage cheese, egg, seasonings, and herbs.
2. Stuff pepper halves with the mixture.
3. Top with grated cheese.
4. Bake at 375°F (190°C) for 25 minutes until golden.

Sauerkrautauflauf mit Käse (Sauerkraut Casserole with Cheese)

Ingredients:

- 500g sauerkraut
- 2 potatoes, thinly sliced
- 200g sausage slices (optional)
- 200ml cream
- 150g grated cheese
- Salt, pepper, caraway seeds

Instructions:

1. Layer sauerkraut, potatoes, and sausage in a baking dish.
2. Season and pour over cream.
3. Top with cheese.
4. Bake at 375°F (190°C) for 35–40 minutes until bubbly and golden.

Käsige Gemüsepfanne (Cheesy Vegetable Skillet)

Ingredients:

- 1 zucchini, sliced
- 1 bell pepper, chopped
- 1 carrot, julienned
- 100g grated cheese
- 1 onion, chopped
- Butter or oil, salt, pepper, herbs

Instructions:

1. Sauté vegetables in a skillet until soft.
2. Season with salt, pepper, and herbs.
3. Sprinkle cheese over the top, cover and cook until melted.
4. Serve as a side or light main dish.

Rahmkäse mit Schnittlauch (Cream Cheese with Chives)

Ingredients:

- 200g Rahmkäse (or substitute with a mild cream cheese)
- 2 tbsp finely chopped chives
- Salt, pepper
- Optional: a splash of milk or cream for smoother texture

Instructions:

1. Stir the Rahmkäse until smooth.
2. Mix in chives, salt, and pepper.
3. Serve chilled as a spread with fresh bread or pretzels.

Toast Hawaii mit Käse (Hawaiian Toast with Cheese)

Ingredients:

- 4 slices of toast
- 4 slices of cooked ham
- 4 pineapple rings
- 4 slices of cheese (Gouda or Emmental)
- Butter

Instructions:

1. Preheat oven to 200°C (390°F).
2. Butter the toast slices, then layer with ham, pineapple, and cheese.
3. Bake on a tray for 8–10 minutes, or until the cheese is melted and golden.
4. Serve hot.

Spiegelei mit Käse überbacken (Cheese-Baked Fried Eggs)

Ingredients:

- 2 eggs
- 50g grated cheese
- Butter or oil
- Salt, pepper

Instructions:

1. Fry the eggs sunny side up in butter or oil.
2. Once whites are set, sprinkle cheese on top.
3. Cover the pan and let the cheese melt over low heat.
4. Serve with toast or potatoes.

Semmelknödel mit Käse (Bread Dumplings with Cheese)

Ingredients:

- 4–5 bread rolls (a day or two old), cubed
- 150ml milk
- 2 eggs
- 100g grated cheese
- 1 small onion, finely chopped
- Parsley, salt, pepper, nutmeg

Instructions:

1. Sauté onion, then mix with bread cubes, milk, eggs, cheese, and seasoning.
2. Let soak 15 minutes. Form dumplings.
3. Boil in salted water for 15–20 minutes.
4. Serve with mushroom gravy or melted butter.

Kürbis-Käse-Gratin (Pumpkin Cheese Gratin)

Ingredients:

- 500g pumpkin, peeled and sliced
- 150g grated cheese (e.g., Gruyère)
- 200ml cream
- 1 garlic clove, minced
- Salt, pepper, nutmeg

Instructions:

1. Preheat oven to 190°C (375°F).
2. Layer pumpkin in a baking dish.
3. Mix cream with garlic and seasoning, pour over.
4. Top with cheese and bake for 25–30 minutes.

Hackbällchen mit Käsefüllung (Cheese-Stuffed Meatballs)

Ingredients:

- 400g ground beef or pork
- 1 egg
- 1 onion, chopped
- 50g breadcrumbs
- 100g cheese cubes
- Salt, pepper, paprika

Instructions:

1. Mix meat, egg, onion, breadcrumbs, and seasoning.
2. Form balls around cheese cubes.
3. Fry or bake at 200°C (390°F) for 20–25 minutes until cooked through.

Käsige Nudelpfanne (Cheesy Pasta Skillet)

Ingredients:

- 300g cooked pasta
- 150g grated cheese
- 1 onion, chopped
- 1 bell pepper, chopped
- 100ml cream or milk
- Butter, salt, pepper, herbs

Instructions:

1. Sauté onion and bell pepper in butter.
2. Add pasta and stir in cream.
3. Stir in cheese until melted.
4. Season and serve hot.

Käsige Zucchini-Küchlein (Cheesy Zucchini Fritters)

Ingredients:

- 2 zucchini, grated and squeezed dry
- 2 eggs
- 100g grated cheese
- 2–3 tbsp flour or breadcrumbs
- Salt, pepper, herbs
- Oil for frying

Instructions:

1. Mix all ingredients into a batter.
2. Heat oil in a pan, drop spoonfuls of batter, flatten slightly.
3. Fry until golden on both sides.
4. Drain on paper towels and serve warm.

www.ingramcontent.com/pod-product-compliance
Lightning Source LLC
LaVergne TN
LVHW081323060526
838201LV00055B/2432